IN COLI

The Walker Family Murder

by

JT HUNTER

IN COLDER BLOOD
The Walker Family Murder

by

JT HUNTER

Copyright and Published by
RJ Parker Publishing, Inc.
09.2016

ISBN-13: 978-1987902143
ISBN-10: 1987902149

http://RJParkerPublishing.com/

Published in the United States of America

Copyrights

While the Publisher is responsible for the sales, marketing and distribution of a book, it is the author's obligation to ensure the accuracy of facts.

Table of Contents

Preface

In 1965, Truman Capote published *In Cold Blood*, a self-styled true account of the November 15, 1959, quadruple murder of a family of four in Holcomb, Kansas. The two men who committed the crime, Richard Eugene Hickock and Perry Edward Smith, had recently been released from prison.

In addition to murdering Herb Clutter, Bonnie Clutter, and their teenaged son and daughter, Hickock and Smith were seasoned con artists and cunning liars. They denied killing another family of four near Sarasota, Florida, approximately a month after the Clutter murders, despite many remarkable similarities between the two crimes.

While *In Cold Blood* provides a fascinating character portrait of Hickock and Smith, Capote's narrative focuses on their involvement in the Clutter family murders.

There is more to their story.

Chapter 1: Their Last Day of Errands

Christine Walker glanced excitedly in the bathroom mirror as she hurried to get ready. Her husband, Cliff, had just surprised her with the news that it was time to trade in their 1952 Plymouth for a newer model, one with more room for their growing family. Thrilled by the prospect of getting a new car, Christine quickly changed into a red-and-white floral dress that complimented her "well-built" body and curvy, Marilyn Monroe-like figure. After a couple of quick touch-ups to her curly, light brown hair, she slipped on a pair of high-heeled shoes and started rounding up their two children. Cliff, a rugged 25-year-old ranch hand, standing about 5'10" and weighing a lean 140 pounds, was already on his way out the door. He was dressed in his typical cowboy attire of Levi's jeans, a denim jacket, brown cowboy boots, and a white cowboy hat.

It was Saturday, December 19, 1959, and with Christmas right around the corner, the Walker family planned a busy day of errands, one that would be highlighted by car shopping in Sarasota. Christine let three-year-old Jimmy wear his cowboy hat so he could look like his father, and she dressed

Debbie, just a month shy of her second birthday, in a blue plaid dress. Christine looked forward to showing off Debbie's newly curled hair, which had been styled at a beauty parlor the day before.

With her friendly smile and outgoing personality, 24-year-old Christine liked meeting new people and going places, even for such seemingly mundane matters as running errands. Aside from the inherent excitement of looking for a new car, she always enjoyed visiting the city, seeing some friends, and simply getting out of the house for a while. There was only so much that could entertain her in their small, sleepy town of Osprey, located in a rural area of Sarasota County in southwestern Florida.

In contrast to Christine, Cliff was more of an introvert, a quiet cowboy-type who had a few close friends, but mainly kept to himself and focused on his family. Well-liked by those who knew him, Cliff would "go out of his way not to offend anyone," and a family member described him as "one of the most wonderful guys you ever met." Although not much of a drinker, Cliff did have one guilty pleasure: a deep-seated affinity for cigarettes. Indeed, his long-time smoking habit had such a hold on him that he would not hesitate making a special trip in the middle of the night to buy a pack of Kools, his cigarette of choice.

Cliff and Christine were both from Arcadia, another small, rural town about 45 miles to the east of Osprey. They had met when Christine was still a teenager attending Arcadia High School. The former Christine Myers had caught Cliff's eye when she was head drum majorette, leading the high school marching band at football games and proudly parading down Main Street, twirling her baton high into the air, using a technique she had perfected through hours of practice with a broomstick at home. Christine and Cliff shared a love of rodeos where she often twirled rope and he tested his skills in calf-roping competitions. Their romance had quickly blossomed, culminating in their marriage in 1954 when Christine was only 19.

Although they married young and they had their share of marriage spats, Cliff and Christine maintained a strong relationship and never wavered in their devotion to each other and their children. Indeed, Christine once remarked to her mother that although her sister lived a more comfortable lifestyle and owned a lot more clothes, "she still hasn't got what I've got. I've got a husband and a happy home."

The Walkers lived in a small, white, wood-frame house in an isolated area at the edge of the Palmer Ranch, situated among a varying assortment of pine trees, oaks, and palmettos, about two miles northeast of town. Commonly referred to as a "line shack," the simple, sparsely furnished "cottage" was similar to other living quarters used by ranch hands in scattered locations around the sprawling 14,000-acre ranch that bounded much of southern Sarasota County. Located off a mixed shell and dirt road that led to Highway 41 at Osprey, the house sat about 100 feet from the Seaboard Line railroad tracks. Although Cliff only earned about $220 a month, the family lived in the house rent-free. It was one of the perks of his job at Palmer Ranch, where he had served as a ranch hand for the past three years, proving to be a dependable, hard-working employee.

Aside from the house's modest furnishings, a few pictures adorned the walls or otherwise decorated the interior of the home. One picture frame held a photo of Cliff on horseback, dressed in a white cowboy hat, a dark-colored, long-sleeved Western shirt, Levi's jeans, and a thick leather belt with a large buckle. Two prize ribbons jutted prominently from his hands.

*****

The Walkers began their Saturday errands in the late morning, leaving their undecorated Christmas tree outside on the front porch. Their first stop was the local IGA store to do some grocery shopping. Always eager to catch up on the latest town gossip, Christine chatted with Thelma Tillis, the store's owner, and mentioned that she was mad at Cliff for getting into a fight with someone the day before. Half an hour later, groceries in hand, the Walkers were on their way to Sarasota to look at cars.

Shortly before noon, the family began browsing at several used car lots as they considered potential trade-ins. At one of the lots, a 1956 Chevy caught their eye, a two-tone model painted green with a white top. They test drove a car at another dealer, Altman Chevrolet, then stopped by Johnny's Hardware and bought hot dogs, sodas, and hot drinks, as well as penny candy and cookies for the kids. Cliff also picked up a little something for himself: a new carton of Kool cigarettes. Cliff's mood, temporarily brightened by his purchase, morphed to one of annoyance when he learned that one of the kids had dropped the keys to the Plymouth out of the window during the test drive at Altman Chevrolet. However, deep down Cliff enjoyed his kids' antics, and by the time they back-tracked to the car dealership to recover the missing keys, his irritation had mostly faded away. The family dropped by Corbett's Garage on Swift Road in Sarasota for a short time period afterward as one of their last errands of the day.

Around 2:00 in the afternoon, the Walkers arrived at Don McLeod's house on Clark Road located at the opposite end of the Palmer Ranch in Sarasota. After some polite conversation, Don and Cliff left to go hunting nearby, leaving Christine and the children in the house to visit with Don's wife,

Lucy. At one point, Christine used the McLeods' telephone to call her uncle, Carl Myers. During the conversation, Lucy overheard Christine mention that she would be "trading" her car.

Cliff and Don McLeod returned to the house about ninety minutes later. Shortly after getting back, they took Cliff's Jeep to the adjacent barn to load some sacks of feed for his bulls. At 3:45 p.m., Christine stopped by the barn in the family's Plymouth.

"The kids want to ride with you in the jeep," she told Cliff, pulling up next to him.

Christine helped Jimmy and Debbie out of the car, and as she prepared to leave, Cliff assured his wife that he would be home soon.

"I'll be right on," he told her.

At 3:50 p.m., Cliff went inside the McLeod home to use their phone, but no one answered the call. Don and Lucy tried to convince him to stay for a while, but after looking at the clock, Cliff commented that he had better get going because it was "almost 4:00."

As Cliff started the Jeep's engine and pulled away, Jimmy waved goodbye to Don McLeod.

"See you later, Uncle Donald!" he yelled with a little boy's infectious smile.

At 3:55, Christine stopped at the Phillips 66 gas station near the intersection of U.S. 41 and Bay Street in Osprey. She stayed for only a few minutes, just long enough to put air in her tires, and then continued on her way home.

About fifteen or twenty minutes later, Howell Crawford waved to Cliff and the kids as they pulled into the same Phillips 66 gas station that Christine had stopped at a little earlier. The sun was beginning to set, giving way to a cloudy, chilly night as an oncoming cold front moved in from the north, its gloomy grey-black clouds growing ominously darker as they approached.

Chapter 2: The Approaching Storm

A few days before the Walker family's busy Saturday of shopping, two men with errands of their own drove south down Highway 27. Recently released from prison, their past crimes had consisted primarily of burglaries and thefts, but lately they had escalated the level of their offenses. The two men had been on the run since committing their most egregious crime, a quadruple murder in cold blood, a month ago and over a thousand miles away. During the early morning hours of November 15, 1959, 28-year-old Richard Eugene Hickock and 31-year-old Perry Edward Smith had broken into a remote farmhouse in the small town of Holcomb, Kansas, and murdered rancher Herb Clutter, his wife Bonnie, and their two teenaged children, Nancy and Kenyon.

Despite the magnitude of their crime, the 5'10", 175-pound Hickock and 5'4", 155-pound Smith were singularly calm as they drove, confident no one would catch them, convinced Kansas authorities would never be able to link them to the killings. After all, they had no prior connection to the Clutters, and they had been careful not to leave any witnesses behind. Hickock had insisted on that part of the crime, reminding Smith on several occasions that he wanted to see "hair on the walls" of the Clutter house. True to the plan, after surprising the Clutter family members in the dead of night, Hickock and Smith tied them up in four different parts of their house, then shot each of them in the head at close range, one by one, with a shotgun.

*****

Born in Kansas City, Kansas, the blonde-haired, blue-eyed Hickock had once been a promising student, but when his family could not afford to send him to college, he gave up on his grades, replacing his books with mechanic's tools instead. Born in Huntington, Nevada, Smith was in many ways Hickock's opposite, brown-haired, brown-eyed, and with a much darker complexion. While neither man had enjoyed anything close to a perfect childhood, Smith had the harsher upbringing of the two due to an abusive father and an alcoholic mother who committed suicide when he was only thirteen. Unlike Hickock, Smith had never married.

In their more recent pasts, both men had suffered serious accidents that left lasting physical and psychological scars. Hickock had a severe car accident in 1950 that left his face slightly disfigured and caused him to occasionally black out. Smith had a damaging motorcycle accident in 1952 that nearly killed him, permanently disfiguring his legs, causing him chronic pain for the rest of his life.

The two men had met while serving prison sentences in the Kansas State Penitentiary: Smith was released on parole in early July, while Hickock had been released on August 13. They reunited in Kansas City, Missouri, three days before driving to Holcomb, Kansas, and killing the Clutters.

*****

A few days after the Clutter murders, Hickock and Smith had fled to Mexico, moving from place to place in that country until they returned to the United States on December 11. After taking a bus to San Diego, the two made their way to Las Vegas, and then hitchhiked to Nebraska and Iowa. It was in Iowa that they acquired the 1956 two-door Chevrolet Bel Air that they now drove. Two-tone in color, Hickock had stolen the car after finding it parked in a barn, and they had been using it ever since. Next, they drove to Kansas City, where they stole a Kansas license plate, tag identification number JO-16212, to replace the existing tag on the stolen Chevy. While in Kansas, they also purchased an Olympic television set by writing a bad check as payment, Hickock's particular criminal specialty.

After travelling through Oklahoma, Arkansas, and Louisiana, they crossed the Florida state line and spent the night of December 16 at a Salvation Army shelter in the Florida Panhandle city of Pensacola. By late morning the next day,

Hickock and Smith had made their way to Tallahassee. They pulled in to the Tip Top Café on U.S. 27 just east of town, and after showing a bill of sale for the bad check purchase, they sold the Olympic television set to the café's owner for $50.00, assuring the buyer that they had some promising job prospects around Tampa and would return in a week or so to buy it back.

After lunch, they turned back onto Highway 27 and stopped at Frosty Mack's Tire Shop, where they exchanged the new tires on their car for $20 cash and a set of used tires. Then they continued on U.S. 27, taking it south toward Miami.

Chapter 3: A Shocking Discovery

Early on the morning of December 20, twenty-nine-year-old Don McLeod roused himself from sleep and quietly dressed in the semi-darkness. Careful not to wake his wife and children, he crept out of the house and stepped outside into the cold, predawn air. Wearing thick clothes, a jacket, and an aviator-style hat with ear flaps, he coaxed a horse into the trailer attached to his GMC pick-up truck, started the engine, and drove west on Clark Road. At U.S. 41, he turned and headed toward Cliff Walker's house. He and Cliff had plans to hunt wild hogs that had recently been spotted on the Palmer Ranch, and the two men had agreed to get an early start.

It was about 5:30 a.m. when McLeod arrived at the Walkers' home. He found the metal cattle gate that served as the main entryway to the property fastened, but not locked. He pulled the gate open and drove through, parking near the silent, unlit house. Christine's car was parked by the interior gate, a patchwork wooden door constructed of wood planks that were nailed together and secured to woven wire fencing mounted on old wooden fence posts. He noticed that Cliff's Jeep was parked between the house and barn near the back gate.

After walking to the back door of the house, McLeod knocked and waited. There was no response. Not a sound issued from the still-dark house. Not a noise penetrated the eerily quiet yard except the faint exhalations of his own chilled breath. A look of bewilderment slowly spread across his face as he realized that Cliff had failed to answer. The two men had been friends for over three years, and on the many prior occasions that they had gone hunting together, Cliff had always been dressed and ready to go when McLeod arrived, waiting to share a pot of hot coffee with him. Amused by the thought that he might have finally caught Cliff asleep, he walked to the bedroom window and tapped on it, gently at first, but then gradually louder and with more urgency. Still no one answered.

Growing concerned that something might not be right, he hurried to the front of the house and found the screen door to the porch unlocked. An undecorated Christmas tree stood sentinel on the porch. Wrapped Christmas presents were arranged neatly below it. McLeod moved forward onto the porch and tried to open the French doors that allowed access to the living room, but they were securely locked. Despite several attempts, he could not get the doors to budge.

Peering through a window to one of the bedrooms, McLeod noticed a faint light flickering inside. The unnerving thought crept into his mind that the Walkers' gas heater might have malfunctioned during the night and asphyxiated the helpless family while they slept.

Moving more urgently, he hastened back to the rear door. Fearing that every second could be the difference between life and death, he cut the mesh screen door with his pocket knife, then unhooked the door latch, opened the back door, and stepped into the house. He turned on the kitchen light and froze in place. Through the kitchen doorway, he could see Christine Walker's bare feet and legs lying motionless on the cold, hardwood floor.

McLeod's heartbeat quickened as he moved closer to Christine's body and saw the extent of her injuries. The vivacious young woman he had joked and laughed with hours before was sprawled on her back in the doorway leading to the dining room, her face battered, her hair discolored with blood. Just beyond her, McLeod could see Cliff lying equally lifeless, flat on his back on the living room floor with little Jimmy curled up beside him. Blood covered the floor on all sides of them. McLeod panicked at the thought that the killer might still be lurking somewhere in the house. He sprinted out of the room in terror, retracing his path through the kitchen and back door.

Knowing that his truck was slowed by the horse trailer attached to it, he jumped into Cliff's Jeep. Relieved to find the keys left in the ignition, he gunned the engine and darted down the road. As he drove, he noticed that the burlap bags of cattle feed that he had helped Cliff load were still in the back of the Jeep. This struck him as odd because he knew that Cliff always unloaded feed as soon as he got home. Something had compelled him to stray from his normal routine and head straight into the house.

McLeod sped back to town intending to call the police from the IGA grocery store on Bay Street. But when he pulled up to use the payphone, he realized that he did not have any money. His mind raced frantically as he tried to figure out what to do. Suddenly, he spotted a woman opening up a nearby restaurant. When she heard the urgency in his voice and saw the desperation in his eyes, she did not hesitate in loaning him a dime.

McLeod rushed back to the payphone and called the Sarasota Police Department. It was approximately 5:45 a.m.

"Some people's been hurt," he exclaimed to the dispatcher on the other end of the line. "I think they're all dead."

The city police department quickly notified the Sarasota County Sheriff's Office, which dispatched all available deputies in the area to respond to the scene.

McLeod paced anxiously at the IGA as he waited for the police to arrive. After what "seemed like an hour," Deputy Russell Mize pulled up in his patrol car.

*****

Decades later, McLeod would be unable to shake the terrible images of the murder scene from his memory.

"I can still see it plain as if it happened right now," he told a reporter grimly. "You've never seen anything so horrible."

The gruesome deaths of the two Walker children were what haunted him the most.

"They were such little fellers," he said tearfully. "They were babies, really."

Chapter 4: Bodies and Blood

A cold rain fell as Deputy Mize accompanied a still visibly shaken McLeod back to the scene of the crime. The bleak drizzle added to the paralyzing feeling of gloom that overcame McLeod as they pulled up to the Walker house. After parking beside Christine's car, Mize walked around to the back of the house and followed the same route that McLeod had taken through the back door. Wary that the perpetrator might still be present, Mize moved cautiously, taking measured steps into the kitchen before making his way into the living room. He tried to brace himself for what awaited him, but the horrific scene still sent a chill down his spine.

Christine Walker's body lay face up on the wooden floor, her head turned a little to the side, resting just outside the doorway between the dining room and living room. Her dress and slip were scrunched together and pushed up around her hips, and her underwear had been pulled down to her lower legs. Both of her arms were stretched out above her head as if she had been dragged to the spot and abandoned there. Her eyes were wide open, as if still experiencing the terrifying moments of her violent death. A pool of blood that had seeped from her head was spread across the floor. A blood-stained towel was wadded up beside her.

A few feet away, Cliff Walker's body lay on the floor in the southeast corner of the living room. His head was tilted slightly toward the French doors that led to the front porch. The doors were closed and locked. Cliff lay flat on his back, still wearing his denim jacket, his right hand resting across his stomach, his left arm extended down in its natural position beside him. Eyes closed, his head was cradled in his cowboy hat, as if he had fallen straight back at the moment of his death. Trails of blood oozed from the lower inside corner of his right eye and from both of his nostrils.

Dressed in a striped shirt and jeans, three-year-old Jimmy lay on the living room floor beside his father. His legs were slightly curled up, bent in at the knees, and he was on his left side, facing away from Cliff with his back against his father's legs, his head toward his father's shins. A thin, white lollipop stick was at his feet, the candy all eaten. A small toy plane was on the floor a few feet away from his head. Blood smears coated the floorboards around him and his head lay in a pool of blood. His eyes were closed, just like his father.

Jimmy had been shot in the head three times: once beneath his right eye, in nearly the same spot that had killed his dad; once in the left eye with the bullet entering between his eyelids, and once in the upper left side of his head. This last shot propelled the bullet completely through his skull, sending it exiting behind his ear. As McLeod later described it, Jimmy's "little brains were running outside of his head."

The boy's green felt cowboy hat was on the floor a few feet from his body, a bullet hole clearly visible in a location that corresponded to where the bullet had entered the side of his head. Gunpowder burns on the hat and evidence of tattooing on Jimmy's right eye indicated that the weapon had been only inches from the boy's head when it was fired. Based on the extensive blood smears on the floor, as well as the angles at which the bullets struck him, investigators theorized that Jimmy had fallen to the floor after being shot the first time, the force of the bullet impact knocking the cowboy hat off of his head. Still alive after the first bullet pierced his head, but suffering immense pain, the scared little boy crawled in panic toward his dad, pleading for help. As Jimmy dragged himself to his already dead father, the killer shot him twice more in the head. The final shot ended his short life as he curled up in terror and agony against his father's body. The little boy who wanted so much to be like his father bore a tragic resemblance to him in death.

Debbie, not yet two years old, had been shot once through the top of the head, near the doorway where Christine's body was found. Bloodstains on the floor indicated that she had crawled over to her mother before the killer fired a bullet straight down into her skull. Strangely, a second bullet hole in Jimmy's green cowboy hat corresponded to this shot in Debbie's skull, suggesting that the killer covered her head with the hat before shooting her, not wanting to see the bullet's violent impact to the little girl's body. After firing that shot, the killer had apparently run out of bullets, evidenced by the fact that one of the recovered shell casings showed two firing pin markings on it in two separate spots. This indicated that the gunman had unknowingly attempted to fire an empty shell, unaware that all of the cartridges had been emptied of bullets.

A trail of blood drops led from the location in the living room where Debbie had been shot, through the kitchen, and into the bathroom where her body was found. The blood trail suggested that Debbie did not die after being shot, and that after running out of bullets, the killer had carried the wounded girl to the bathroom to finish her off. There he placed Debbie in the tub, stuffed a sock in the bathtub drain to serve as a plug, and filled the tub with about four inches of water. Then he held her head underwater until she drowned.

That was where Mize found her. Her tiny body, hair still curled, lay face down in the bathtub. Next to the tub, colorful depictions of cartoon penguins adorned the cabinet of the bathroom sink. The penguins were comically combing their hair and brushing their teeth, no doubt meant to encourage the kids to use good hygiene habits. In front of the sink, the trail of blood drops from the hallway terminated on the edge of the tub beside Debbie's body. The scene was etched into Mize's memory forever.

"It was a sight I'll never forget," he murmured sadly years later.

As other deputies arrived and viewed the bloody crime scene, they were also "visibly shaken by what they saw." Even Sheriff Ross Boyer, an officer with well over a decade of law enforcement experience, found it difficult to absorb the disturbing images.

*****

In light of the obvious violence that had occurred in the small house, investigators noticed some unusual aspects of the crime scene. The furniture, sparse as it was, seemed undisturbed, and it appeared that, after arriving home, Christine had taken the time to hang up her purse in the kitchen. It hung there still, seemingly untouched by the killer. Christine had also felt comfortable enough after arriving home to put away the groceries purchased during the family's errands that day. She had even placed a Christmas card from Lucy McLeod on top of the refrigerator to display it.

The location of Christine's car was equally puzzling. According to her family and friends, she nearly always parked immediately to the left of the entry to the inner gate. She preferred parking there because, after getting out of the car, she only needed to take a few steps to walk through the gate and into the house. The fact that on the day of the murders she had parked two car widths away from the walk-in gate led investigators to theorize that another vehicle was parked in Christine's usual spot when she arrived home. Upon finding the person or persons parked in her spot beside the gate, Christine, who "never met a stranger," would likely have "invited them in to be friendly," telling them they could wait inside the house until Cliff returned. It seemed equally reasonable to conclude that Christine was expecting, or had at least previously met, whoever was waiting in her spot.

*****

Deputy Billy Blackburn, who arrived at the crime scene shortly after Deputy Mize, searched within the fenced area of the Walker property for signs of automobile tracks that may have been left behind by a vehicle other than those of the police officers responding to the scene. Although Blackburn could not locate any tracks, he was unable to conclude with any certainty whether another vehicle had been there. Indeed, by the time Blackburn arrived, Deputy Mize had already parked in the spot directly beside Christine's car, the exact spot where the killers' vehicle may have been parked when Christine arrived home the day of the murders. That being the case, it seemed reasonable that any tire tracks left by the killer had been obliterated by Mize's patrol car.

*****

Based on their ballistics analysis and reconstruction of the murders, sheriff's investigators believed that Christine was shot first, while lying on the bed in Jimmy's room immediately after being raped. Cliff was shot next, in "sniper fashion" from about ten feet away, as he walked into the house. The killer had most likely crouched behind a partially opened bedroom door to ambush Cliff as he stepped through the double French doors. The killer shot Jimmy third, and then either shot Debbie, or killed Christine with a second shot to the head directly from above. The second shot, the one that took Christine's life, had been fired straight down, the bullet entering the top of her head and lodging at the base of her brain. Based on other evidence at the scene, including tissue fragments on the right pocket of Cliff's shirt, the killing shot had most likely been fired execution style as she knelt over her fallen husband.

Investigators later discovered that this second bullet differed from all of the other shots fired during the murders. The weight and grain of that bullet revealed it to be a .32 caliber slug, as opposed to the .22 caliber shots fired throughout the rest of the crime scene. Empty .22 cartridges were found alongside each of the four victims.

Investigators theorized that Cliff and the two children pulled up to the house in the Jeep at around 4:45 p.m., disturbing Christine's attacker during the sexual assault. Unaware of any danger, Cliff never thought of grabbing his loaded rifle and left it outside in the Jeep. Attempting to enter the house according to his normal habit of using the back door, Cliff had found it locked, so he walked around to the front of the house and entered through the front porch. As he opened the French doors and stepped into the living room, the cold-blooded killer struck. Before Cliff could even begin to comprehend what was happening, a single bullet struck him in the corner of his right eye. He died almost instantly and fell straight back onto the floor.

A bloody high-heeled shoe was found on the front porch, where Christine, a "strong woman physically," most likely used it as a weapon while trying to defend herself against her attacker's initial assault. Bruises and abrasions on Christine's face, forehead, and arm indicated that the killer struck her multiple times while she desperately struggled to fight him off. As they wrestled and fought, Christine's attacker forced her into Jimmy's bedroom and onto the bed where he sexually assaulted her. Once he finished raping her, he intended to kill Christine with a shot to the head, but the bullet was off target. Instead of killing her, it only grazed the top of her head, causing a two-inch long laceration before striking the wall behind the bed and falling into the window. Pieces of Christine's hair and skull fragments found in the wall about four feet above the bed supported this reconstruction of events. Another blood-stained high-heeled shoe, a match to the one on the front porch, lay on the floor by the doorway into the bedroom, evidencing that Christine had continued trying to fight off her assailant as they moved into that room.

An examination of Christine's clothing revealed a seminal fluid stain on the lower rear portion of her underwear. Sheriff's Bureau lab analysts concluded that, due to the condition of the stain and the fact that a number of intact sperm were isolated from the stain, Christine had worn the underwear "very little, if at all, after the deposit of the seminal fluid".

*****

Bloodstains present on both sides of the glass-paned French doors indicated that they had initially been open during the commission of the crimes and were then closed by the killer. The fact that considerably more stains were present on the outside of the doors caused investigators to conclude that most of the shootings occurred while the doors were in their opened position, extended outward into the living room, likely due to Cliff having opened them as he entered the house. The door and doorway connecting the living room to the dining room were also splattered with blood, and the killer had apparently used a quilt blanket to wipe blood from Christine's legs after dragging her body approximately three feet across the living room floor. Lacking any clear-cut reason, investigators could only speculate as to why the killer had cleaned off Christine's legs.

The bathroom floor and tub containing Debbie's body were both spattered with blood, and what were believed to be fingerprints were recovered from the tub's hot water faucet handle and the bathroom mirror. Much later in the investigation, analysts determined that the prints were more likely partial palm prints, not fingerprints as had long been assumed.

In Jimmy's bedroom, although a quilt was pulled up over the pillow on his bed, investigators discovered blood under the pillow when they pulled back the quilt. Strangely, the killer had taken the time to cover the blood with the quilt, as if that act might somehow undo what had happened.

A red cellophane strip from a cigarette package was found lying on the dining room floor in the midst of several bloodstains. This suggested that the killer had smoked one of his own cigarettes since the Walkers were known to smoke only Kool cigarettes, a brand that did not have a red strip in its packaging. Cash and a pocket knife were missing from Cliff's pockets, and the carton of Kool cigarettes that he had purchased during the family's errands was also stolen. Yet, numerous Christmas presents were left untouched.

Bloody boot imprints were found near the door of Jimmy's bedroom, near the foot of the bed, and near Christine's body. However, forensic examiners were unable to determine the type of boot or shoe that made the imprints.

*****

Investigating officers found several photographs among the Walkers' personal items in the house, including a photo of Christine wearing a short-sleeved shirt, light colored shorts, and white drum-majorette boots with tassels. The back of the photo contained a handwritten note in pencil: "I will always love you with all my heart." Another photograph, this one of the entire family, had a handwritten notation on the back: "August 28, 1958, Sonny's Photos, Arcadia, Florida. Christine, Cliff, Jimmy, Debbie Walker. Our third Christmas on the Palmer Ranch."

Tragically, it would be a Christmas none of them lived to see.

For Cliff's uncle, Rob Walker, the killings of Jimmy and Debbie were particularly hard to understand. "I don't know how a human being could shoot a child and put her in a bathtub," he said sadly.

*****

On Monday, December 21, Christine's mother received a letter from her daughter that had been postmarked in Osprey on December 18 at 6:00 p.m., less than twenty-four hours before Christine was brutally murdered:

> *Dear Mother:*
>
> *I will write you a line or two. We are all fine. How is everyone over there? I am sorry that I haven't wrote sooner but I have been so busy trying to get everything done before Christmas.*
>
> *Mother we will be over on Christmas eve night, so I will be so glad when it comes so I can see you again. I bought Debbie a pretty red and white dress for Christmas. She sure does look nice in it. I am going to have her hair fixed today. How is Charlie getting along? Tell him hello for me. Cliff caught 3 big hogs yesterday in the pasture. Boy I have a lot to tell you when I see you. One of my friends is making me a pretty dress and it fits like a tea.*

Love,

Christine

What Christine meant by having "a lot to tell" her mother, and whether it had anything to do with her death, no one would ever know.

Chapter 5: Too Many Suspects

The shocking murder of the family of four dominated the front page of the *Sarasota Herald-Tribune's* December 21 edition under the frightening heading, "Osprey Family Wiped Out." The story continued on the paper's inside pages with the equally disturbing header, "Killer's Bullets Annihilate Family" along with graphic photos of sheriff's deputies standing beside the bodies of Cliff and Jimmy Walker and staring grimly down at Christine's battered body. Beneath the continued story, a photograph of a little girl sitting in Santa's lap and smiling during a VFW Christmas party provided a stark contrast to the unimaginable crime, which had so suddenly shattered the holiday atmosphere, abruptly intruding upon a community's shared sense of peace and goodwill.

News of the murders quickly swept through the small-town community of Osprey. People who had lived in Osprey all of their lives without ever locking their doors started locking them now. Long-time residents began sleeping with guns by their beds, fearful of being the next victim. Parents stopped letting their children play outdoors alone, while neighbors who had greeted each other every day with a wave and a smile, now secretly began to suspect each other of committing the crime. Even family members began to look at one another suspiciously.

On Tuesday, December 22, a funeral service was held for the four murder victims at Robarts Funeral Home in Arcadia. Nearly 500 friends and relatives attended the service, after which Cliff, Christine, Jimmy, and Debbie were buried side by side in Oak Ridge Cemetery in their home town of Arcadia.

The Palmer Ranch offered a substantial reward for information leading to the capture of the Walker family's killer. Deedee Faltin, the Palmer Ranch supervisor who had hired Cliff, summed up the feeling of loss, describing him as the "nicest kind of cracker boy you could ask for. He didn't drink. He didn't carouse. We were all just stunned. You just couldn't believe anybody would have any bad feeling toward Cliff and his family."

*****

Over the frantic days and weeks following the murders, detectives investigated an ever-widening web of leads, interviewing suspect after suspect as rumors and suspicion swirled among the residents of the previously peaceful town. Osprey resident Sam Holland summed up the suspicious atmosphere surrounding the case.

"There's been a lot of wild people that lived in Osprey," he said. "There's been a lot of good people too. There was a lot of different opinions about what happened."

On December 24, State Attorney Mack Smiley stressed that while investigators had no "definite leads" in the case, they were following up every potentially relevant tip no matter how inconsequential it might seem.

"We're not looking for any one person in particular," Smiley said.

Amidst the tempest of police activity, a handful of individuals rose to the top of the Sheriff's Office's list of suspects: Elbert Walker, Cliff's cousin; Emmitt Spencer, a serial killer who confessed to the crime; Curtis McCall, a high school boyfriend of Christine Walker; Wilbur Tooker, one of the Walker family's closest neighbors; and Don McCleod, the family friend who had discovered the bodies.

*****

Years later, while discussing the scene of the crime, which he called a "hell of a mess" because deputies had allowed too many people to access the Walkers' house, Elbert Walker recalled the cloud of suspicion that rapidly rose around him.

"When I showed up there on Saturday morning, I was automatically guilty," he said, a tone of resentment clearly evident in his voice.

Elbert had quickly become a suspect because several witnesses reported that he had long been enamored with Christine and, in addition to this purported attraction, he had acted strangely after the murders. He broke down in near hysterics outside the Walker house when a deputy told him that he could not go inside because all of the family members were dead. Earlier that day, he acted like he did not know how to get to their house, asking for directions at a nearby gas station, despite the fact that he had lived there with Cliff and Christine for at least a month after getting out of the Army in 1958. And during the family's funeral service, he wailed inconsolably, fainted twice, and had to be carried out. Many who witnessed the events thought that he was faking and had "put on a show" in an attempt to deflect suspicion from himself. Cliff's brother, Clarence, candidly told detectives that Elbert was the "type of person who would commit a crime of this nature."

Elbert remained a suspect despite passing several lie detector tests over the years. It would take half a century before DNA would clear his name, when testing that compared Elbert's DNA profile to a DNA sample taken from semen in Christine's underwear showed that he did not sexually assault her shortly before her death.

After reviewing the results of the DNA testing, Detective Ron Albritton pronounced Elbert innocent.

"Common sense says the person who assaulted her was the murderer, and Elbert didn't assault her," he said matter-of-factly.

*****

While on death row at the Florida State Prison in Raiford, Florida, for a double homicide he committed two weeks after the Walkers were killed, serial killer Emmitt Monroe Spencer claimed to have killed the Walker family with the help of his girlfriend, Mary Hampton, and a phantom individual he referred to as "Johnny." Spencer, dubbed the "Dream Slayer" because authorities found murder victims after he dreamed about murders and then described his dreams, claimed that Hampton had spotted Christine Walker in Osprey outside the grocery store, and then he, Hampton, and "Johnny" followed her home.

When Spencer walked up to the front porch, Christine tried to hold the door shut, but he forced his way in and punched her several times in the face in an attempt to subdue her. He and Christine struggled until he forced her into a small bedroom, where he held her down while Mary Hampton "performed an unnatural sex act on her." When Christine threatened them that her husband would kill them when he came home, they were alerted to his imminent arrival. Spencer waited in ambush, and shot Cliff from outside the small bedroom as he came into the house. They killed Christine next, then the two children. Spencer, who claimed to have taken part in at least 26 murders in total, asserted that the motive for the Walker murders was "sex and robbery."

On December 4, 1960, Sheriff Boyer interviewed Spencer in prison but found that he could only provide general information about the murders, nothing more specific than what he could have gleaned from reading various newspaper accounts of the crime. Spencer offered Boyer an easy way to close the file, telling him to "write out what you want me to sign about the Walker murders and I will sign it." If true, Spencer's confession would have been a welcomed way for Boyer to declare the case solved, but his confession simply was not credible.

"There were a lot of questions he could not answer," Boyer said after interviewing him. "If I am wrong, I will be the first to admit it, but right now I think Spencer is a liar."

Additionally, investigation of Spencer's whereabouts during the pertinent time period revealed that in 1959 he and Hampton had been in California on Christmas Day, and they were arrested in Crestview, Florida, on December 31, while on their way back from California. After assessing

Spencer's travels and confirmed locations during the month of December, Sheriff Boyer concluded that he could not have been in Osprey on December 19 and thus could not have killed the Walkers.

*****

Twenty-one-year-old Curtis McCall was known to have a quick temper, and some who knew him described him as a "no-good, trouble-making sort of person." McCall was said to have dated Christine Walker during high school, and after her marriage to Cliff, Christine jokingly referred to McCall as "my boyfriend." He had worked for a time at the Arcadia Police Department and later as a dispatcher for the Florida Highway Patrol in Fort Myers. He also worked at the Food Fair grocery store in Sarasota where Christine sometimes shopped. McCall's own cousin told investigators he knew "for a fact" that Christine and McCall were having an affair. Some speculated that McCall had been the cause of two miscarriages Christine had while married to Cliff, one in April 1959 and one approximately two months before her death.

One witness recalled seeing Christine and McCall at a secluded spot together in McCall's car just a few days before the murders. Another remembered that two weeks prior to the killings, on a day when Cliff Walker was at a rodeo in Wauchula competing in a calf-roping event, Christine had shown up in Arcadia looking for McCall, telling people that it was "very important" that she talk to him that day.

McCall owned a .22 pistol at the time of the Walker murders, and witnesses reported that subsequent to the murders, he lost weight, seemed "very nervous," and had problems keeping a steady job.

On July 14, 1961, Sheriff Boyer, accompanied by one of his deputies, travelled to Americus, Georgia, to interview McCall, who had relocated there for a job as a construction foreman. McCall came across as being "very nervous" and denied having ever dated Christine, either before or after her marriage to Cliff Walker. He also denied that Christine Walker had ever visited him at work in Sarasota, or that he had been in his car with Christine in the days before the murder. He admitted to owning a .22 pistol at the time of the murders but said that he had long since sold it to someone whose name he could not remember. McCall agreed to take a lie detector test, and although the test indicated that he was "extremely nervous," it suggested that he had generally told the truth about his relationship with Christine. The sole question that he appeared to have falsely denied was, "Have you withheld any information from the law enforcement officers about the Walker murder?" Despite the red flag raised by McCall's response to this question, based on the fact that he had passed the rest of the lie detector test, Sheriff

Boyer decided that McCall was not responsible for the Walker murders.

*****

Sixty-five-year-old Wilbur Tooker, a retired railroad worker, lived about a mile away from the Walker house on Osprey Siding Road. As their closest neighbor, he had often visited them during their years living on the ranch. Don McLeod stated that he had personally seen Tooker drop by the Walker house forty or fifty times over the years. According to McLeod, Tooker usually parked his car by the railroad tracks outside the fence and then walked to the house.

One of Tooker's friends said that he seemed infatuated by Christine and constantly talked about her. The infatuation had manifested in other ways too. During some of his visits to the Walker house, Tooker had made unwelcome advances towards Christine, one time going so far as grabbing her and trying to force her to kiss him. When Cliff found out about it, he had to be restrained from going after Tooker, and he forbid him from ever coming to the house again.

Sometime between 5:00 and 7:00 p.m. on the evening of the murders, Tooker ate dinner with a friend of his, a dentist who lived in Sarasota. Tooker had no such alibi for the 4:00 to 5:00 time period in which the Walkers were actually killed.

*****

Like Elbert Walker, Don McLeod quickly became a suspect and remained one for decades despite passing several polygraph tests. McLeod was interrogated at the scene of the crime the morning he discovered the family's bodies, questioned by State Attorney Mack Smiley for nearly an hour in a car right outside the Walker house. He was also the first suspect to take a lie detector test about the murders, a test he easily passed the same day. But it took DNA testing in the 21st Century to finally clear McLeod's name when a 2004 analysis showed that his DNA did not match the suspect profile generated from the semen stain in Christine Walker's underwear.

*****

During its decades of on-again, off-again investigation of the Walker case, the Sarasota Sheriff's Office would investigate nearly 600 suspects. None led to a resolution of the case.

*****

A couple of months after the murders, Osprey resident Pearl Strickland and her daughter found two shirts and a skirt hidden in a shed on Strickland's property, which was located less than two miles from the Walker house. One of the shirts had obvious blood stains on it in several places.

The following day, Cliff Walker's sister identified the shirt as having belonged to Cliff.

A blouse and handkerchief were subsequently discovered in the same location. Both were also blood-stained.

*****

One year into the investigation, Boyer referred to the Walker murders as the "most vicious crime" he could recall in his career as a law enforcement officer, and it was one that he pledged to solve.

"This case still has top priority in my office. The only time we will quit working on the case is when the murderer is brought to justice," he vowed. "After a year of reading and studying our investigation, it seems like a dream," Boyer said. "It seems that I can see the whole story unfold – except the man who pulled the trigger and walked away."

Boyer's wife reported that he had been so focused on solving the crime that he canceled a planned Christmas party shortly afterward, declaring, "We're not going to have any parties until this case is solved."

*****

As the years passed with the identity of the Walkers' killer still unknown, new cases and emergency calls increasingly demanded the attention of the sheriff and his deputies. However, Boyer made sure that the investigation of the Walker case remained active. On December 18, 1963, nearly four years after the Walker family murders, he directed the release of a statement:

> *Not a day goes by but we of the Sarasota County Sheriff's Office feel that we are moving closer to the killer. During these four years of investigation dozens of suspects have been questioned and released; hundreds of persons have been interrogated. Scores of clues, real and worthless, have been run down.*
>
> . . . . .
>
> *No case in the history of this office has ever been investigated so thoroughly for so long by as many officers as we have assigned to this crime. We are confident that the Walker murders will not go unsolved.*

Cognizant of rumors that continued to run rampant in the community, Sheriff Boyer added a personal comment, stating

> We haven't stopped and we aren't going to until the case is solved.

There is nothing I or my men would rather do than break this one. Not only as law officers but as men horrified by what we saw. Many people have formed their own conclusions as to who did the killing, why, and how. Speculations and hastily drawn conclusions will not suffice in this case. Only cold, hard evidence will ever bring the killer to court.

Photos

Source: Sarasota County Sheriff's Office Case File

Map showing Arcadia, Sarasota, Osprey and Miami, Florida

Cliff, Christine, Jimmy, and Debbie Walker outside their home in Osprey, Florida

Exterior of Walker house showing entry gate

Outside of Walker house the day their bodies were discovered

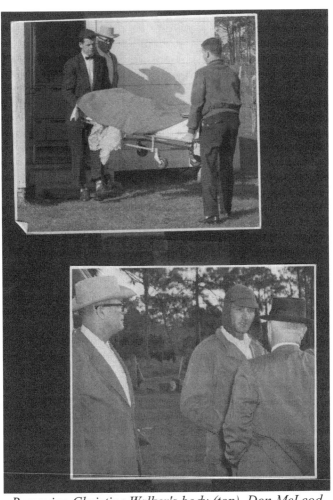

Removing Christine Walker's body (top) Don McLeod (bottom)

Bodies of Cliff, Christine, and Jimmy Walker

Bodies of Cliff, Christine, and Jimmy Walker (2)

Different view of bodies of Cliff, Christine, and Jimmy Walker

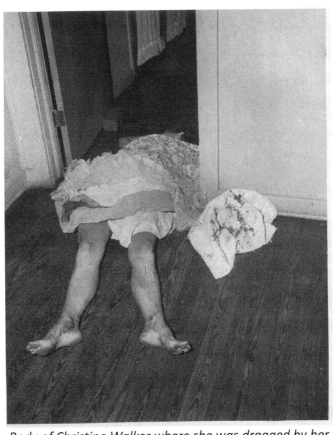

Body of Christine Walker where she was dragged by her killer

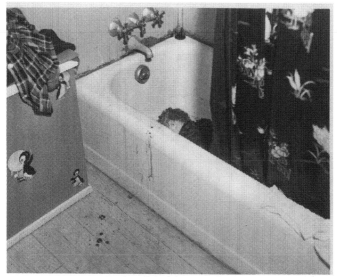

Body of Debbie Walker

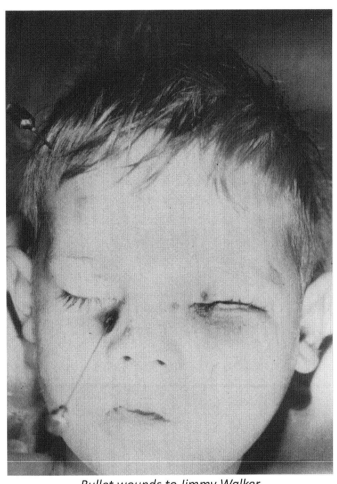

Bullet wounds to Jimmy Walker

Sheriff Ross Boyer pointing to bloody boot imprint

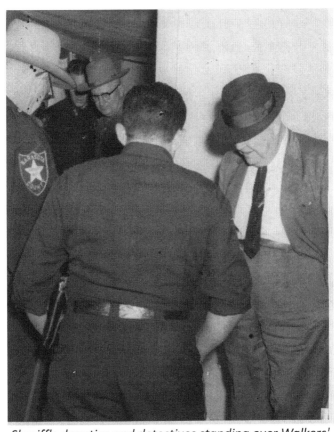

Sheriff's deputies and detectives standing over Walkers' bodies

Trail of blood leading to Debbie Walker's body

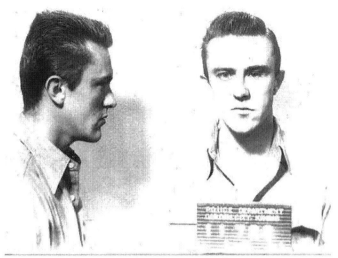

Booking photo of Dick Hickock after his arrest

Booking photo of Perry Smith after his arrest

Chapter 6: New Blood, Renewed Direction

Sarasota County Sheriff Ross Boyer died in 1973.   The twenty-year lawman who witnessed firsthand the brutal crime scene and bloodied bodies of Cliff and Christine and their two young children had handled many key aspects of the early investigation himself. Just prior to his death, Boyer told his wife that the one thing he wished he could have accomplished with his life was solving the Walker case.

*****

In 1981, someone else with a vested interest in identifying the killer took over the investigation. Fifty-year-old Ron Albritton, a distant cousin to Cliff Walker who joined the department a few years after Boyer's death and worked his way up to detective, presided over periodic spurts of investigative activity in the frequently inactive cold case for the next two decades.

*****

On August 5, 1994, an anonymous caller left a voice message on the answering machine of a Sheriff's Office detective. The caller advised that she wanted to provide information about a "possible murder that occurred in Osprey, Florida, many years ago," but she was scared and too frightened to give her name or phone number. She explained that she worked as a bartender in Stroudsburg, Pennsylvania, and that during her work shift the previous night, one of her regular customers, a "white male in his 60s" inexplicably began to cry while talking to her. She asked him why he was crying, and he told her that when he was a young man he had killed "some people" in Osprey, Florida. He said that Osprey was near Tampa and he mentioned the name "Walker".

The caller said that she thought the customer was a "gun buff" who did odd jobs around town. She said she would get the name and vehicle tag number of the customer's car and then call back after 3:00 p.m. on August 9 with the information. However, she never contacted the Sheriff's Office again, and subsequent attempts to track her down were unsuccessful. Even a series of stories about the anonymous call, requesting the public's help in identifying the caller, which were printed in Pennsylvania newspapers at the urging of the Sarasota Sheriff's Office, failed to generate any new information. The unnamed caller and her remorseful unknown customer faded back into anonymity.

Curtis McCall, Christine Walker's high school boyfriend who failed a polygraph question asking if he withheld any information about the

Walker murders, would have been 56 years old at the time of the anonymous tipster's call.

*****

Detective Albritton's tenure in charge of the Walker case file included an important period of activity when new DNA samples were provided to the Florida Department of Law Enforcement for analysis. The process generated a DNA profile for Christine's attacker in 2004, which eventually eliminated more than thirty top suspects, including Elbert Walker and Don McLeod, whose DNA did not match the suspect DNA profile attributed to Christine's killer.

In 2007, Albritton retired from the Sheriff's Office, sharing Ross Boyer's burden of having failed to solve the Walker case and being unable to bring closure to the community. It was a disappointment he hoped to see remedied by his successor.

"To the people who grew up in this community, to the relatives of those families – all these people deserve that closure," he said emphatically.

*****

Beginning in September 2007, thirty-seven-year-old Kimberly McGath took over the Walker case. Detective McGath, a four-year veteran of the force who earned the nickname "Bulldog" due to her tenacity and determination, requested the infamous cold case that many believed unsolvable out of a deeply held desire to identify the killer and bring closure to the victims' surviving family members, as well as to Don McLeod and many others who had been waiting so long for justice.

"The family compels me to do the work," McGath explained. "They deserve those answers."

McGath began her work on the case by familiarizing herself with the file, a mammoth task considering the reams of documents it contained: over thirty-three volumes of documents in all. Day after day, she spent countless hours reviewing and organizing the relevant reports, newspaper articles, crime scene photographs, and witness testimony. McGath read many of the documents multiple times, scouring them for overlooked leads or forgotten nuggets of evidence that might warrant devoting renewed resources to the long-cold case.

While sifting through hundreds of case file documents, McGath began to home in on assorted pieces of information that intuitively seemed connected.

"Some things started jumping out at me," she said.

McGath decided to focus her attention on one particular aspect of the Walker family's last day alive: their whereabouts and activities as they shopped for a new car.

*****

As she researched the files, McGath noticed that J.W. Thornton, the operator of AAA Motors Used Car Lot on Ringling Boulevard in Sarasota, had informed investigators that Cliff and Christine Walker and their two children came to the lot on December 19 to look at some of the dealer's vehicles. The Walker family stayed at the lot until shortly before noon, at which time they mentioned that they were going to Altman's Chevrolet. They returned to AAA Motors at about 12:40 p.m. and test drove one of the cars, then left the used car lot at 1:00 p.m. but returned again at 1:30 to look for a set of car keys that one of their children had thrown out of the window during the test drive.

McGath also noted a DeSoto County Sheriff's report reflecting that Cliff Walker had been at Altman Chevrolet in Sarasota on the day of the murders "making a car trade with Harry Rauchenberger," one of the dealership's salesmen. According to the salesman, the car that Cliff wanted to trade for was a 1956 Chevrolet, 210 model, two-toned with a greenish bottom and white top. The report also stated that, following the murders, Rauchenberger attended the Walker family's funeral, although he did not appear to have known them prior to their visit to the dealership that day.

Rauchenberger later denied that he attended the funeral.

As she reviewed the witness testimony, McGath wondered whether the Walkers' errands that fateful December day had attracted the attention of two fugitives of the law, two men who had backgrounds in automobile painting and body work, and who frequented gas stations and used car dealerships looking for odd jobs. McGath discovered that, despite their representations to the contrary, substantial evidence supported that Dick Hickock and Perry Smith were prowling the streets and automobile dealerships of Sarasota at the same time that the Walkers were in town car shopping.

December 17, 1959

The owner of a tire shop reported that on December 17, 1959, just two days before the Walker family was murdered, two men matching Hickock's and Smith's descriptions pulled up to the curb of the Frosty Mack Tire Company in Tallahassee. They said that they wanted to sell the new whitewall tires on their car for cash and a replacement set of used tires. After one of the men produced a bill of sale for the tires reflecting that they had paid $60 for them, the tire shop's owner agreed to buy the tires for $20 and exchange them for used ones. As the two men departed, one of the workers at the tire shop asked them where they were going. They answered that they were going "hunting."

According to Ted Smith, the operator of a gas station in Sarasota located at Cattlemen's Road and Fruitville Road, two men who matched photographs and physical descriptions of Hickock and Smith came to his station later that afternoon asking if anyone needed auto painting. One of them claimed to be a "car painter" and inquired about automobile paint shops in the area.

Another witness, G.W. Moye, reported that around 4:30 p.m. on the same day, a man matching Perry Smith's photograph came to Moye's home driving a car with an out-of-state license plate. The man asked if Moye would pay him to repair a dent in the fender of Moye's car. He told Moye that he and his partner, a blond-haired man who remained in their car, did odd jobs and automobile body work, stating, "Mister, we do body work and we noticed that your fender is bent. We do good work and we would like to fix your fender".

In her investigative report, McGath noted that Perry Smith had worked for a time as a car painter and Dick Hickock had experience working as an automobile mechanic and a used car salesman.

December 18

As verified by hotel records, on December 18 shortly before dark, Hickock and Smith checked into the Somerset Hotel on Ocean Drive in Miami Beach. The hotel clerk on duty took their payment for one week's rent and filled out a receipt to provide a record of the transaction.

December 19

The morning of December 19, Hickock and Smith appeared at the front desk of the Somerset Hotel and requested a return of the unused portion of the week's rent money that they had paid in advance as they "intended to leave the hotel." Their request for a refund was denied, and no one at the hotel recalled seeing the two men after that.

Kathy Rudis and Mary Reynolds, saleswomen in W.T. Grant's Department Store in Sarasota on Tamiami Trail near U.S. 41, reported seeing Hickock and Smith shopping in the store on December 19. Although Rudis could not recall the exact time, it had to have been during her work shift between 10:00 a.m. and sometime in the afternoon. She distinctly remembered seeing the two men because of their odd appearance: they both wore coats that did not match their pants, their hair was long, and their shoes were missing laces. The department store was located only about seven miles away from the Walker home.

McGath noted that Hickock and Smith had shopped in a department store for various supplies the day before they committed the Clutter family murders.

December 20

Several witnesses near Arcadia positively identified Hickock and Smith as having stopped in the area on December 20, asking for directions on how to bypass Arcadia – Cliff and Christine Walker's hometown – but still connect with Highway 27. The witnesses stated that the two men were driving a dark-colored car and they noticed that the taller, blond man had scratches on his face.

Buck Wever reported that, between 10 and 11 a.m. on December 20, a man he described as approximately 20-25 years old, 6'1", 165 pounds, blond-haired with a "scratched-up" face and small "round" cuts and bruises on his forehead the "size of a dime," had stopped at his gas station. The man came into the station in a hurry and asked how to get to the Bair's Den restaurant via the town of Nocatee. The man had been adamant that he did not want to travel through Arcadia. Wever also noticed another man who remained sitting in the car that the man with the scratched-up face had been driving. After some quick research, McGath found that the Bair's Den restaurant had been located on U.S. 27 at the intersection of State Road 70 in December of 1959.

McGath deemed it significant that Wever reported his December 20 encounter with the two men the very next day, on December 21, before Florida authorities were aware that Hickock and Smith were wanted for the Clutter family murders or that they were even in the state. It was also well before the *Sarasota Herald Tribune* published photographs of the two men on January 24, 1960, under the caption, "Have you seen them?" Since law enforcement did not know the two fugitives were in Florida, Wever could not have known it either. Yet, his description of the man with the scratched-up face was uncanny in its resemblance to Hickock.

Wever also reported that the Chevrolet the two men were driving had the number "16" as part of its license plate number, a significant fact since the stolen Chevy Bel Air that Hickock and Smith drove while they were in Florida had a stolen license plate with tag number JO-16212. Moreover, Wever later picked Hickock out of a photographic lineup and confirmed that he was the tall blond with the "scratched up face" who had stopped at his gas station on December 20.

A witness at another gas station, Holland's Pure Oil located at Magnolia and U.S. 17 in DeSoto County about forty miles from the Walker family home, reported that two white males came to the station between 10 and 11 a.m. the day after the Walker murders and asked how to get to the Bair's Den. According to the witness, the man who got out of the car to ask directions had dark hair and wore a cowboy hat. The other man, who stayed in the car, had a "badly scratched-up" face.

The witnesses' reports about the taller of the two men having a scratched-up face with "round" cuts and bruises the "size of a dime" particularly piqued McGath's interest. After all, crime scene evidence indicated that Christine Walker, who was wearing high-heeled shoes, had fought ferociously as she attempted to defend herself from her attacker. McGath also noted a *St. Petersburg Times* article from December 22, 1959, entitled "Brutal Killer of 4 May Have Cut Face," which stated that the Walker family's killer "may be marked by cuts from a woman's high-heeled shoe."

Another witness, Dick Brown at Nocatee Cities Service in DeSoto County, reported that around 11:00 a.m. the same day, two white males drove up to the station, bought candy and drinks, and asked how to get to U.S. 27. Brown described one of the men as being 6'1", 165 pounds, with blond hair and a "badly scratched-up face." He described the other man as being shorter and older, with dark-colored hair and a cowboy hat.

McGath noted in her report that Hickock had a known affinity for candy and that he had purchased some candy at a gas station the day before murdering the Clutter family.

*****

Upon reviewing Richard Hickock's and Perry Smith's inmate cards, as well as Hickock's Kansas Bureau of Investigation (KBI) card, McGath confirmed that their height, weight, and hair colors matched the descriptions given by the witnesses who reported encountering two men asking for directions on December 20.

The multiple sightings of Hickcock and Smith at gas stations and car lots also rang true to the two men's history of seeking odd jobs painting or fixing vehicles, as well as their habit of visiting gas stations and car lots. Indeed, as McGath noted in her final investigative report, when Hickock and Smith were identified as the prime suspects in the Clutter murders, the Kansas Bureau of Investigation issued an "All-Points Bulletin" notifying all car lot owners of their descriptions.

The more she studied the case file, the more McGath became convinced that it was not mere coincidence that multiple witnesses reported seeing Hickock and Smith around the Sarasota area both during the days leading up to the Walker murders as well as shortly afterward.

Other Evidence Pointing to Hickock and Smith

In addition to the numerous sightings of the two men around the area, McGath noted that two suspicious hairs had been found at the scene of the Walker murders. Both hairs were tested and determined to be inconsistent with any members of the Walker family. A dark hair had been discovered in the bathroom near Debbie's body, and it was undisputed that Perry Smith had dark hair. The other suspicious hair was a long, blond hair that had been recovered from inside Christine's dress. Dick Hickock, who by his own admission had a history of sexual assaults, had the same type of hair.

Very early in the investigation, Sheriff Boyer had requested that Hickock's and Smith's fingerprints be checked against the latent impressions recovered at the scene of the murders from the Walkers' bathtub faucet handle. On January 29, 1960, the Director of the Florida Sheriff's Bureau (predecessor of the Florida Department of Law Enforcement) advised that he had received copies of the two men's fingerprints from the FBI, but they did not match the impressions found at the crime scene. However, subsequent analysis determined that the prints recovered from the Walkers' bathroom were most likely a partial palm print, rather than fingerprints. Similarly, both Hickock and Smith took polygraph tests about the Walker murder in 1960, and both men passed the tests. However, in 1987, the polygraph expert for the Sarasota Sheriff's Office concluded that polygraphs given decades earlier were extremely unreliable and essentially worthless, an opinion shared by most contemporary polygraph experts.

Detective McGath also found it significant that Christine Walker had parked her car in an unusual location shortly before her murder, indicating that another vehicle was already parked in her customary parking spot. McGath highlighted a DeSoto County Sheriff's report that included testimony from a Seaboard Railway brake foreman testifying that he had seen a 1956 two-tone dark green and white Chevrolet parked in front of the Walker home the day before the murders, while a former sheriff stated that the 1956 Chevrolet was parked at the Walker home on the actual day of the murders.

McGath noted that at least two friends of the Walker family testified that Christine kept a .22 pistol on the highest shelf of the closet in Jimmy Walker's bedroom. She recalled that one of Christine's blood-stained shoes was found behind the drape of that closet, suggesting that after being confronted by her attacker, Christine may have tried to retrieve the gun to defend herself. The fact that she was shot by a .22 caliber gun in the same room suggested the possibility that her attacker had wrestled the gun away from Christine and then used it against her.

McGath also highlighted the fact that when Las Vegas Police officers arrested Hickock and Smith on December 30, 1959, a pocketknife was among the items that Smith was carrying on his person. The knife had a fruit-tree design and a silver blade. The design and blade were strikingly similar to witnesses' memories of Cliff Walker's pocketknife, which was reported as missing after the murders.

Chapter 7:   A New Theory Emerges

Based on the totality of the evidence tracing the Walkers' movements during the hours leading up to their murder, and combining it with Hickcock's and Smith's appearances around the area, McGath theorized that the two men had encountered the Walker family while they were in Sarasota car shopping. Assuming that the parties' paths had indeed crossed, it was reasonable to conclude that the two seasoned con artists learned, either directly from the Walkers themselves or from one of the car salesmen they had been dealing with, that Cliff Walker was interested in trading for a car substantially similar to Hickcock's and Smith's stolen 1956 Chevy Bel Air. Armed with that knowledge, Hickock and Smith convinced Cliff to trade for the Bel Air, either as a way to obtain some much-needed cash or as a ploy to rob him. The parties then arranged to meet at the Walkers' house later that afternoon to finalize the trade. During this discussion, Christine could have easily caught Hickock's eye, arousing interest that would later prove fatal. Since Christine mentioned "trading" the Walkers' Plymouth during her telephone conversation at the McLeod's house, and Cliff subsequently commented to the McLeods about needing to leave because it was "nearly 4:00,"

McGath surmised that Hickock and Smith arrived at the Walker house for their appointment sometime between 3:00 and 4:00 p.m.

Taking into account when Christine left the McLeods' house and her brief stop to put air in her tires at the Phillips 66 gas station in Osprey, she would have arrived home at approximately 4:08 p.m., finding Hickcock and Smith parked in her usual spot next to the inner entry gate. This theory is supported by testimony from a witness, Chuck Downs, who flew over the Walkers' home in his small plane at 4:20 p.m. and saw two vehicles parked in front of the house.

Considering Christine's upbringing and southern hospitality, it would have been wholly within her character to invite Hickock and Smith into the house to wait for Cliff to return to further discuss or finalize a potential deal for trading cars. Once inside the house with her, Hickock's physical attraction to Christine could have taken over his thinking, his sexual inclinations pushing aside any prior intentions of striking a deal for the car. Indeed, after his arrest for the Clutter family murder, Hickock revealed that his primary motivation for breaking into the Clutter home was to rape Nancy Clutter, and he confessed to having frequent desires to sexually assault young women. Moreover, as described in Capote's novel, *In Cold Blood*, Perry Smith "almost had a fist fight" in order to stop Hickock from raping Nancy Clutter, a confrontation that he said he "wouldn't care to repeat." Not wanting to "repeat that particular test of strength" may have kept him from trying to stop Hickock from raping Christine Walker. McGath also knew that during his trial for the Clutter murders, psychiatrists who examined Hickock concluded that he suffered uncontrollable impulses and lacked a normal ability to tolerate frustration, a trait which often resulted in his committing antisocial acts, including violent ones.

"I think it was Hickock losing control, wanting to rape Christine, that could have triggered the events that day," McGath explained.

At 4:28, approximately twenty minutes after Christine's arrival, Cliff and the children pulled up in the Jeep and parked in the back of the house, oblivious to what awaited them inside.

*****

Hickock's attempt at an alibi did nothing to diminish McGath's belief in her theory of his involvement in the Walker murders. Hickock told KBI investigators that he and Smith had stayed in Miami Beach at the Somerset Hotel from December 21 through December 26, and that when they finally left Miami they drove straight through the state without stopping anywhere overnight. However, his story was subsequently shown to be untrue. For one thing, hotel records unequivocally established that the two men checked into the Somerset Hotel on December 18. If Hickock misled investigators about the date they checked in, it stood to reason that he also lied about when they left, and no one at the Somerset Hotel recalled seeing Hickock or Smith after the morning of December 19.

In addition, the two men were seen in Sarasota later that day, and they were spotted by several witnesses near Osprey, Florida, the following day, on December 20. A few days later, on the evening of December 22 or 23, they returned to the Tip Top Café on Highway 27 east of Tallahassee. They told the owner, the same witness to whom they had sold a television set on December 17 on their way south, that they were "flat broke" because the job they had lined up in Tampa "had not turned out." Additionally, on December 24, when according to Hickock they were still in Miami Beach, the two fugitives sold two dolls wrapped in Christmas paper to Reverend John Gibson in Delhi, Louisiana, for gas money. (Witnesses in Florida testified that Christine Walker had gone Christmas shopping shortly before her murder, and baby dolls would have been a likely choice for gifts for her daughter Debbie.) Six days later, just before the New Year, Hickcock and Smith were in Nevada. Thanks to a tip from an informant who knew about their plan to rob the Clutter family, they were arrested in Las Vegas for the Clutter murders, an offense they had committed only six weeks earlier, a crime that shared remarkable similarities with the Walker family murders.

*****

In her final investigative report submitted on May 4, 2015, McGath compiled an extensive list of similarities between the unsolved Walker family murder and the Clutter killings that were known to have been committed by Hickock and Smith:

(a) Both families were murdered on a Saturday night in their own homes.

(b) Both crimes were quadruple murders of a father, mother, son, and daughter.

(c) The Clutter family members were murdered in order of father, son, daughter, and mother, while the Walker family members were killed in order of father, son, then most likely daughter and mother.

(d) No witnesses were left alive at either crime scene.

(e) Both crimes occurred in an isolated, rural setting on a farm or ranch.

(f) All of the family members were shot in the head in both cases.

(g) All male members of both families were shot in the face.

(h) All female members of both families were shot in the back, side, or top of their heads.

(i) There was evidence that the adult women were raped at both scenes. Blood Type A semen was found on the clothing of the adult women in both cases: on the "rear" of Bonnie Clutter's nightgown, and on the "rear" of Christine Walker's underwear.

(j) There were hair and head tissue fragments on the walls of the houses from murdered females in both cases, and Hickock told Smith prior to the Clutter murder that "I want to see hair on those walls."

(k) Boot prints were found at both crime scenes, with Smith leaving a "cat's paw design" boot print in the Clutter basement and a similar "cat's paw design" print being found in the Walker living room.

(l) Boot prints were found near a window in the Walker home and Smith admitted that he looked out of a window in the Clutter home during the crime to see if anyone was coming.

(m) The boot prints in both the Clutter and Walker cases made stronger impressions on the right side of the boot than the left, and Perry Smith was known to walk with an unusual gait due to leg injuries he sustained from a motorcycle accident.

(n) Petty cash and miscellaneous low-value items, such as binoculars (Clutter home) and a carving set (Walker home), were taken from both homes.

(o) Jewelry was not taken at either crime scene.

(p) The lights were turned off in both homes.

(q) Hickock was a chain smoker, and a cellophane wrapper for cigarettes that did not match the Kool brand which Cliff Walker smoked exclusively was found near Christine's body. A cigarette butt was also found at the Clutter crime scene.

(q) Hickock and Smith buried evidence in a field after the Clutter murders, and bloody clothing was found in a nearby field after the Walker murders.

(r) Smith followed the news on the radio and in newspapers about both the Clutter and Walker murders.

(s) "Undoing" acts by the killer at the Walker crime scene – pulling the quilt over the bloody pillow on Jimmy's bed, and covering Debbie's head with her brother's cowboy hat before shooting her – were similar to actions taken by Perry Smith during the Clutter killings, such as tucking Nancy Clutter in her bed and placing a pillow under Kenyon Clutter's head before killing them.

McGath also noted that Cliff and Jimmy Walker were both shot directly in the eyes, while Herb and Kenyon Clutter were shot in the face. She thought this might be another connection since Dick Hickock had been temporarily blinded after his automobile accident in 1950, and he donated his eyes for transplant after his death.

Additionally, McGath recalled that Perry Smith claimed that while he was housed in a children's shelter operated by the Salvation Army, one of the shelter's nurses forced him into a tub of ice-cold water and held him underwater until he turned blue, nearly drowning him. McGath believed that Debbie Walker's drowning by being held face down in the bathtub might have been a case of the psychological condition of Identification with the Aggressor, whereby Perry Smith *identified* with the power figure of the nurse who held him under ice-cold bath water when he was a child. Indeed, during Smith's trial for the Clutter killings, a widely respected psychiatrist concluded that he suffered from schizophrenic episodes in which he was prone to commit violent acts while in a "trancelike state." The psychiatrist specifically compared Smith to a similarly disturbed individual who had drowned a young girl by holding her head under water.

Combined with Hickock and Smith being spotted near the Osprey area, both a few days before the December 19 murder of the Walker family as well as the day after the crime, it all added up, at the least, to an extraordinary and startling coincidence.

Chapter 8: The Circumstances of Evidence

Despite all of the unusual similarities and incriminating coincidences between the Clutter and Walker family murders, nothing in the Walker case file gave an indication that anyone from the Sarasota Sheriff's Office had ever interviewed Hickock or Smith about the Walker killings. McGath could not help but lament this missed opportunity. She knew from experience that the first interview with a suspect constitutes a crucial time period for obtaining candor since it is when they are most vulnerable, before the passage of time allows them to distance themselves from their crimes and create false alibis. After their arrest, the initial interview of Hickock and Smith had been conducted by members of the Las Vegas Police Department, who had no inkling that the two men might be connected to a quadruple murder on the other side of the country in Florida. Even subsequent interviews of Hickock and Smith conducted by the Kansas Bureau of Investigation had focused on the Clutter case, with no mention of the Walker murders until much later in the process.

McGath also knew that her task had been made more difficult due to other mistakes committed by investigators early in the case. Indeed, since Sheriff Boyer did not have a crime scene team in 1959, he allowed liberal access to the Walker home after the bodies were discovered, actively enlisting press photographers to take pictures inside the house and permitting reporters to wander through the site. It was also likely that one of the first deputies to respond to the site had inadvertently destroyed tire tracks left behind by the killers.

*****

Convinced that Hickock and Smith committed the Walker murders, but lacking direct evidence that could conclusively tie them to the crime, McGath turned to the ever-evolving field of forensic DNA analysis. During early 2012, McGath made a series of unsuccessful attempts to locate a relative of Dick Hickock who would be willing to provide DNA samples that would allow comparison testing with the evidence recovered at the scene of the Walker murders. She was also frustrated by the inability to obtain palm prints of Hickock or Smith to compare against the partial palm print recovered from the bathtub faucet handle in the Walker home.

One promising lead that developed on the DNA front soon turned into another dead end. A KBI agent had managed to obtain a DNA profile for one of Hickock's purported children, a son named D.R. Although D.R. had declined to voluntarily provide a DNA sample, the KBI agent he met with to discuss the matter was able to procure his profile from a Styrofoam cup that D.R. had used during their meeting. Unfortunately, subsequent analysis showed that the DNA profile taken from the cup was not consistent with the suspect profile obtained from Christine Walker's underwear. Disappointing as this news was, it did not weaken McGath's resolve to exhaust all available avenues to prove her theory. As explained by the KBI, there were many possibilities for the negative results, including that D.R. was not really the biological child of Hickock, or that the Styrofoam cup had been contaminated either in storage or during the testing process. Another possibility was that the suspect sample from Christine Walker's underwear was itself contaminated.

In light of the uncertainty surrounding D.R.'s DNA profile, McGath decided that she needed to go straight to the sources: she would try to get DNA directly from the remains of Dick Hickock and Perry Smith. In early November, using a court order template provided by the KBI, she started writing the probable cause narrative to be filed in support of a proposed order from a Kansas court that would allow her to exhume Hickock's and Smith's bodies from their Kansas graves.

McGath knew there was no guarantee that usable DNA could be extracted from the two men's long-buried bodies. After all, they had been decomposing in their graves for nearly half a century. Nonetheless, she believed that any chance of success warranted trying to bring closure to Cliff and Christine's surviving family members.

"It's absolutely possible" to obtain usable DNA, McGath explained. "It depends on all kinds of circumstances. The soil conditions, the weather, what type of casket it is in. We will have no idea until we get out there."

The fact that Hickock and Smith were buried in Kansas offered McGath greater hope of success because it considerably increased the odds of being able to extract usable DNA. She knew that the DNA deterioration process is slowed in bodies buried in higher elevations and away from excessive heat and moisture.

*****

On November 14, 2012, in the midst of McGath's efforts to obtain DNA profiles for Hickock and Smith, Cliff Walker's niece contacted her with information about Cliff and Christine's marriage certificate. The marriage certificate was a key item that had been missing from the Walkers' personal possessions for more than fifty years. Though long believed to have been stolen from the house by the Walkers' killer, Cliff's niece gave McGath the surprising news that the marriage certificate had turned up among items recently given to her by another family member. The fact that the marriage certificate had not been taken by the Walkers' killer cast some doubt on the long-held theory that the killer was someone who personally knew Cliff and Christine and resented their being together. It weakened an interpretation of the evidence suggesting that the crime had been committed by a jilted lover or jealous former boyfriend.

*****

On December 10, McGath completed a proposed court order to exhume the bodies of Hickock and Smith, and six days later she caught a Delta Airlines flight to Kansas City, Missouri, accompanied by Sarasota Sheriff's Office videographer Jeffrey Blossom. After arriving in Kansas City, they rented a car and drove to Leavenworth County, Kansas, the location of the cemetery in which Hickock and Smith had been buried after their execution. On December 17, McGath and Blossom met Kansas Bureau of Investigation Special Agent Micky Rantz at the Leavenworth County Courthouse. The trio then presented the proposed exhumation order to district court Judge Gunnar Sundby. Judge Sundby reviewed the order and signed it, granting permission to exhume Hickock's and Smith's bodies for purposes of obtaining hair, molar, and femur samples. Since a Kansas warrant authorized the exhumation, any samples obtained would be sent to a Kansas laboratory, the KBI laboratory in Great Bend, for examination and DNA testing.

Shortly after sunrise on December 18, under mild, clear skies, McGath, Blossom, Rantz, KBI Assistant Director Kyle Smith, Special Agent in Charge Bill Delaney, and other KBI personnel assembled at Mount Muncie Cemetery in Lansing, Kansas, more than 1,300 miles away from the site of the Walker murders. It was exactly 53 years to the day that Hickock and Smith had checked into the Somerset Hotel in Miami Beach, and nearly 53 years to the day that Cliff, Christine, Jimmy, and Debbie Walker were murdered.

Since Lansing Police had previously barricaded the cemetery's entrance in preparation for the exhumation, the team of Kansas and Florida investigators stood together as the sole onlookers in the cemetery. McGath and the others watched as a backhoe began digging up the cold ground of a gently sloping hill at Section 34, Row 29, graves 43 and 44, the spots where the two convicted killers had been buried after being hanged in a Lansing prison warehouse on April 14, 1965, almost half a century earlier. When no family members claimed the killers' bodies, they were placed in plain, cheap coffins and deposited under the dirt in their simple burial plots, all of it paid for with tax dollars from the people of Kansas.

When the backhoe had excavated enough of the long-undisturbed earth covering Perry Smith's grave, members of a KBI Crime response team converged on the coffin and chiseled away at the seal securing the cement lid. After breaking through the seal and removing the lid, they took molar and hair samples from Smith's skull, noting pieces of a black cloth material on his face that appeared to be remnants of the executioner's hood that he had been wearing when he was hanged. After taking the samples from Smith's skull, the team collected samples from his femur bones as well. Then they repeated the process with Hickock's grave.

After both exhumations were completed, the coffin lids were re-secured and the backhoe re-buried the bodies, confining them once again to the darkness of the grave. By the time the team of investigators left the cemetery around noon, an area of fresh dirt spread neatly over Hickock's and Smith's graves gave the only indication that anything out of the ordinary had occurred.

*****

On February 5, 2013, McGath answered her phone to find Special Agent Rantz on the line. He had good news and bad news, and something in between. The good news was that KBI laboratory personnel had been able to obtain a DNA profile from Perry Smith's femur bone. The bad news was that the test results revealed that Smith's profile did not match the suspect profile in the Walker case. The other news Rantz shared was that KBI analysts had not been able to obtain a DNA profile for Dick Hickock, and they were planning on sending Hickock's femur bone and molars to a private laboratory for analysis to see if a DNA profile could be extracted using the equipment and techniques employed by that facility.

Kyle Smith, Deputy Director of the KBI, pointed out that the many decades Hickock's and Smith's bodies had spent buried underground were not helping matters.

"The challenge in this particular case is the age of the material," Smith said. "There are some practical difficulties, that's what we're running into."

Smith mentioned that Florida law enforcement had been interested in renewing the investigation of Hickock and Smith at various times over the decades, but the existing DNA technology had not made it feasible until now. He also explained the KBI's reasons for assisting with the Florida case.

"Our interest is in providing closure to the Walker family," he remarked, before adding, "Obviously, there's a lot of historical interest as well." By "historical interest," he meant the potential ramifications that DNA testing could have with respect to Truman Capote's novel about the Clutter family murder.

"The analysis is not completed," he stressed. "We are still trying."

Smith also emphasized that the DNA analysis would take time and the examination for the Walker case would not take precedence over Kansas crimes that KBI lab personnel were already working on.

Asked when a final analysis of Hickock's and Smith's samples might be completed, Smith could only speculate.

"Ideally, the earliest is in a couple of weeks," he said.

Detective McGath was not surprised. She had anticipated a lengthy process, and she was prepared to wait, no matter what the timetable.

"On cold cases, you have to be very, very patient," she acknowledged before reiterating her resolve. "My gut tells me that we're on the right track."

*****

Almost six months later, on August 1, McGath received and eagerly reviewed the final results of the KBI analysis, as well as the DNA results produced by the private laboratory that KBI had enlisted, Paternity Testing Corporation. After sifting through pages of complex data, McGath discerned the ultimate findings: the tests were still inconclusive.

Although discouraged that a positive DNA match had not been made, McGath took some measure of comfort in the fact that the tests had not exonerated the Clutter killers either. She noted that both sources contained contaminated results, including some of Perry Smith's profiles that had somehow ended up being classified as "female" and one such profile which was determined to be that of the serologist who had conducted the testing on Smith's femur bone.

Disappointed with the inconsistencies of the DNA profiles and exacerbated by the contamination issues, McGath contacted a serology supervisor at the Florida Department of Law Enforcement to ascertain whether the DNA suspect profile in the Walker case might be contaminated as well. After analyzing the data, the serology supervisor confirmed that the majority of the suspect DNA profile that had been used in the Walker investigation for decades actually belonged to Christine Walker, not her unknown attacker. Although he was not responsible for the fundamental error of analysis, the serology supervisor apologized that such a basic mistake had been made.

A forensic supervisor informed McGath that if she provided Hickock's and Smith's boots for analysis, he would be able to make a direct comparison to determine whether the two men had been at the Walker house. He assured her that footwear impression evidence is "very reliable," with some wear pattern comparisons considered to be "as reliable as fingerprints."

Following her discussion with the forensic supervisor, McGath requested permission to try to obtain Hickock's and Smith's boots from the KBI. On August 12, 2013, as the final log entry for her final investigative report, she recorded that her request to seek access to the boots was "not approved."

Chapter 9: Awaiting Closure

Throughout her life, Christine Walker's niece, Wendi Cascarella, had always tried to live up to her family's memories of Christine, especially her "sweet and giving," "kind-hearted" personality. But inside she harbored deep-seated resentment that her aunt had been prematurely taken away from them. It thus came as no surprise that Cascarella found herself drawn to working in law enforcement by becoming a corrections officer, perhaps compelled to do so by silent pleas for justice from Christine's spirit, which Cascarella believes watches over her.

"Hickock and Smith did it! I know it," Cascarella says emphatically. "Cops have a gut feeling, and I know it in my heart of hearts. The DNA is just crossing the t's and dotting the i's."

*****

Don McLeod, the man who had the misfortune of discovering the Walker family's bloodied bodies on a cold, dark December morning, hoped that the DNA testing of Hickock and Smith would at last bring certainty and closure to the case. Worn down by decades of investigation, whispered accusations, and accusing eyes, and haunted by the horrific images of the Walkers' lifeless bodies,

McLeod's deep feelings of disgust for their killers still remains.

"Whoever they were, they were cold-blooded sons of bitches," he says bitterly.

*****

Detective Kim McGath believes that "overwhelming circumstantial evidence" implicates Hickock and Smith in the Walker family murder, a belief apparently shared by the Leavenworth County judge who found that probable cause existed to conclude they committed the crime. Nonetheless, DNA inconsistencies, incomplete genetic profiles, and contamination issues prevented McGath from being able to prove it beyond a reasonable doubt. Disappointed to her core to have "exhausted the extent of scientific testing available today" without definitively identifying the Walker family's killer, McGath reluctantly inactivated the case "until new information becomes available," or until more advanced technology and techniques for DNA analysis allow a clear-cut determination of whether Dick Hickock and Perry Smith were in the Walker house on December 19, 1959.

In announcing that the case would again be relegated to inactive status, Sarasota County Sheriff's spokeswoman Wendy Rose made it clear that while "some uncertainty remains," based on the "totality of the evidence," sheriff's investigators still consider Hickock and Smith to be the "most viable suspects" in the Walker family murders.

*****

The case may again go cold, but Wendi Cascarella insists that the Walkers "will never be forgotten." Although the closure so desperately desired by the surviving family members remains out of reach, Cascarella cannot be doubted when she promises that Cliff, Christine, Jimmy, and Debbie will "forever be in all of our hearts."

Epilogue

In his monumental "true crime" novel, *In Cold Blood*, Truman Capote wrote that Dick Hickock and Perry Smith were in Miami Beach from December 20 to December 26, 1959. Yet, the evidence gathered by the Sarasota Sheriff's Office and other investigators disproves this account of Hickock's and Smith's whereabouts. Capote wrote that the two men were staying in a Tallahassee hotel on December 19, 1959, the night of the Walker murders. Yet, multiple witnesses reported seeing them in the Sarasota area, approximately 325 miles away, on December 19 as well as on the following day.

Capote's account of Hickock's and Smith's activities during the pertinent time period includes a passage describing how Smith learned of the Walker family murders by reading an article about them in the *Miami Herald* while lounging in Miami Beach on Christmas Day. As conveyed by Capote in his novel, Smith expressed his amazement at the crime and then exclaimed that a copy-cat killer must have murdered the Walkers after reading about the Clutter killings that he and Hickock had committed a little more than a month earlier. However, Sarasota Sheriff's Office investigators learned that the *Miami Herald* ran no such story in any December 25 edition of the paper. In response to Smith's claim about a copy-cat killer, Hickock purportedly just grinned, shrugged his shoulders, and sauntered down to the shoreline, perhaps amused by the discrepancy between what he knew to be true and Smith's attempt to deflect what Capote called the "exceptional coincidences" between the two shocking crimes.

Capote also wrote that Hickock and Smith each took a lie detector test regarding the Walker murders on January 20, 1960, and that both tests were "decisively negative." However, McGath found that the tests were actually administered several months later, on or about April Fool's Day. Moreover, in 1987, a polygraph expert for the Sarasota Sheriff's Office opined that lie detector tests administered during the 1960s and earlier decades were essentially worthless due to their inherent unreliability. Other polygraph experts have similarly referred to tests given in the 1960s as "primitive and unreliable."

Aside from the multiple inaccuracies contained in Capote's novel, there is a remarkable lack of discussion about the Walker murders, other than a few short passages in the text. It is widely acknowledged that Capote developed a close, personal relationship with the two Clutter family killers while writing *In Cold Blood*, and that he became particularly attached to Perry Smith.

Additionally, Capote admitted with exasperation that he could not have a proper ending for the story, and therefore could not complete his novel, until Hickock and Smith were executed. Capote was no doubt well aware that implicating them in the Walker murders would bring another trial and with it a lengthy delay in their execution, and correspondingly, a considerable delay in the resolution of Capote's story.

One wonders whether, in the interests of completing his novel, Capote chose to remain ignorant of Hickock's and Smith's ties to the Walker case, or even deliberately downplayed their connections to the crime.

About the Author

JT Hunter is an attorney with over fourteen years of experience practicing law, including criminal law and appeals, and he has significant training in criminal investigation techniques. He is also a college professor in Florida where his teaching interests focus on the intersection of criminal psychology, law, and literature.

JT is the bestselling author of *The Devil In The Darkness*, *The Vampire Next Door: The True Story of The Vampire Rapist John Crutchley* and *The Country Boy Killer: The True Story of Serial Killer Cody Legebokoff*

RJ PARKER PUBLISHING PRESENTS

DEVIL IN THE DARKNESS

The True Story of Serial Killer Israel Keyes

BESTSELLING AUTHOR
JT HUNTER

He was a hard-working small business owner, an Army veteran, an attentive lover, and a doting father. But he was also something more, something sinister. A master of deception, he was a rapist, arsonist, and bank robber, and a new breed of serial killer, one who studied other killers to perfect his craft. He methodically buried kill-kits containing his tools of murder years before returning to reclaim them. Viewing the entire country as his hunting grounds, he often flew across the country to distant locations where he would rent a car and drive hundreds or even thousands of miles before randomly selecting his victims. Such were the methods and madness of serial killer Israel Keyes. Such were the demands of the 'Devil in the Darkness'.

Amazon Links - eBook | Paperback | Audiobook

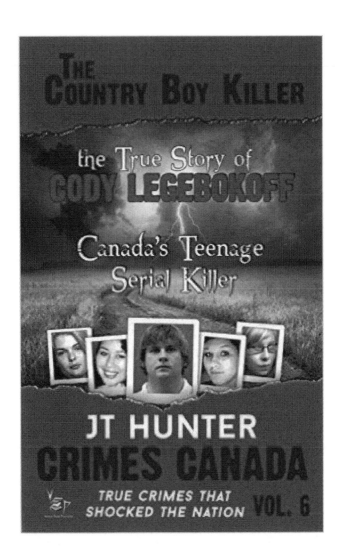

THE
COUNTRY BOY KILLER

the True Story of
CODY LEGEBOKOFF

Canada's Teenage
Serial Killer

JT HUNTER
CRIMES CANADA
TRUE CRIMES THAT
SHOCKED THE NATION   VOL. 6

He was the friendly, baby-faced, Canadian boy next door. He came from a loving, caring, and well-respected family. Blessed with good looks and backwoods country charm, he was popular with his peers, and although an accident at birth left permanent nerve damage in one of his arms, he excelled in sports. A self-proclaimed "die hard" Calgary Flames fan, he played competitive junior hockey and competed on his school's snowboarding team. And he enjoyed the typical simple pleasures of a boy growing up in the country: camping, hunting, and fishing with family and friends. But he also enjoyed brutally murdering women, and he would become one of the youngest serial killers in Canadian history.

Amazon Links - eBook | Paperback | Audiobook

#1 Bestseller in True Crime

The Vampire Next Door

the
TRUE STORY
of the
*VAMPIRE
RAPIST*

www.rjparkerpublishing.com

BESTSELLING TRUE CRIME AUTHOR

JT HUNTER

While he stalked the streets hunting his unsuspecting victims, the residents of a quiet Florida town slept soundly, oblivious to the dark creature in their midst, unaware of the vampire next door.

John Crutchley seemed to be living the American Dream. Good-looking and blessed with a genius level IQ, he had a prestigious, white-collar job at a prominent government defense contractor, where he held top secret security clearance and handled projects for NASA and the Pentagon. To all outward appearances, he was a hard-working, successful family man with a lavish new house, a devoted wife, and a healthy young son.

But he concealed a hidden side of his personality, a dark secret tied to a hunger for blood and the overriding need to kill. As one of the most prolific serial killers in American history, Crutchley committed at least twelve murders, and possibly nearly three dozen. His IQ eclipses that of Ted Bundy, and his body count may have as well.

Amazon Links - eBook | Paperback | Audiobook

RJ Parker Publishing, Inc.

Experience a thought-provoking and engrossing read with books from RJ Parker Publishing. Featuring the work of crime writer and publisher RJ Parker, as well as many other authors, our company features exciting True CRIME and CRIME Fiction books in eBook, Paperback, and Audiobook editions.

www.RJPARKERPUBLISHING.com

and

rjpp.ca/RJ-PARKER-BOOKS

Verified Facebook Fan Page

https://www.Facebook.com/RJParkerPublishing

References

The following sources were consulted in whole or in part in researching and writing this novel:

1. Sarasota County Sheriff's Office case file regarding the Walker family murder (Case No. 59-4756/07-83553) (December 1959 – May 2015), consisting of investigator reports, notes and summaries of witness interviews, Florida Sheriff's Bureau/Florida Department of Law Enforcement correspondence and reports, emails, and other documents relating to the investigation.

2. Recorded interviews of suspects and witnesses conducted by Sheriff's Office detectives.

3. Physical evidence relating to the Walker murders, as maintained in the Sarasota Sheriff's Office evidence vault.

4. Crime scene photographs.

5. Newspaper articles regarding the Walker family murder, the exhumation of the bodies of Dick Hickock and Perry Smith, and DNA testing of suspects, as reported in the *Sarasota Herald Tribune*, the *Sarasota Journal*, *The Sarasota News*, the *Tampa Bay*

Times, *The Wall Street Journal*, *The Brandenton Times*, the *Wichita Eagle*, *The Washington Post*, and other news media sources (time period spanning December 1959 through August 2013).

6. *In Cold Blood* by Truman Capote.

7. Email and phone conversations with Detective Kimberly McGath.

40357475R00066

Made in the USA
San Bernardino, CA
18 October 2016